Life Takes Detours

A Memoir

Julie McGlone
Artist, Writer, Educator
Member Florida Writers Association

Life Takes Detours

Copyright © 2008 by Julie McGlone

ISBN13: 978-1478326038
ISBN10: 1478326034

Printed in the United States of America

Julie McGlone

Acknowledgements

The publishing of this book would not have been possible without the guidance of Phil Wolfson and Lorraine Harris. I am indebted to them for the publishing advice and hours of editing. Thank you, Phil and Lorraine, for your generosity of spirit.

In addition, to my husband Charlie—you *ARE* the story of my life. Every good thing I have accomplished is because of your love and encouragement.

Introduction

When I was a little girl, I would watch my brothers open their Christmas gifts. With several brothers, there were several "boy toys" in the pile. I would open my one gift under the tree that had been wrapped. It was usually a doll.

Although I liked that gift, I would silently vow that one day it would be my turn. One day, I would treat myself.

As a working mother raising my family, I would start my day at 6:00 AM and often go past midnight. I would look into the mirror and silently promise myself that one day it would be my turn. One day I would take time for *me*.

That time has come. I no longer delay gratification, waiting for just the right reason. I no longer take small nibbles at life—I gobble!

That doesn't mean that I buy material goods for myself. It means that I look at life and see possibilities, not limitations.

And that is the spirit I hope I have instilled in my family.

This memoir addresses experiences for you to enjoy and learn from. My life has taken detours on the high road and detours on the low road. But everything has led me to this point.

To my family and friends and anyone who will listen, I say

Life is short.
Don't let the world civilize you too much.
Forgive quickly. Carrying grudges only *hurts you.*
Take the ones you love into your arms and *let them know how much they mean to you.*
Laugh uncontrollably—I mean a real *belly laugh.*
And never regret anything that made you *smile.*

Once I Was Two

My mother was forty-two when she gave birth to me. The doctor and my father had gone to the corner bar to celebrate, when they received a frantic phone call from my Aunt Jule to return to the house immediately.

"There's another one coming!"

With the lack of prenatal testing in 1947, a second child had not been predicted. Twenty minutes later, along came my twin brother, Paul. The two of us, at eight pounds each, made a robust pair. We were dubbed "Sis" and "Junior."

He was able to lose the nickname when he reached six-foot-four; mine has stayed with me until this day. We shared a tandem baby coach, playpen, and hand-me-down toys, and were inseparable companions.

In a Catholic school classroom, I could find him through a sea of strange faces. When Sister Mary Francis decided I should be moved up a grade, she whispered, "If you pass this test, you will go on to second grade." *Was that*

1

supposed to be an incentive? Leave Junior for more strangers?

I was ushered to a desk in the cloakroom and given a timed test of my reading and arithmetic abilities. You can guess the outcome. That was my first experience with dumbing down.

Summers were great fun on my uncle's farm. We fed the animals, rode the tractor, played football in the fields, and picked the juiciest peaches and raspberries I've ever had. Standing on the fence to the pigpen, Paul was beating his chest in his best Tarzan imitation when he fell in.

No automatic washer and dryer in those days. The stinky, muddy clothes were washed in a tub of water and hung out the car window on a stick. Paul and I giggled as he was wrapped in my aunt's blanket for the long ride home.

Everything they say about twins is true.

Even as we got older, we experienced similar trials and tribulations from thousands of miles apart and could usually sense what was going on in each other's lives.

On a Friday afternoon in the spring of 1968, I broke my ankle playing volleyball in college. Equally competitive, Paul broke the same right ankle playing basketball in Germany that day.

When he was having marital problems in Kentucky several years later, he never called to discuss them. I just knew. One day I left a message on his cell phone that said it all: "Head north." He would know what I meant.

Once a friend suggested that he was looking for a woman like me. Hardly. Women were drawn to him like bears to honey. He just always picked the skinny blondes with gold ankle bracelets, bearing no resemblance to me. Besides, I carry enough guilt around. I don't need that burden.

Finally, when he was diagnosed with cancer and hospitalized, he confided in my husband, Charlie, his best friend. I was driving around for days thinking, "Mayo Clinic … Mayo Clinic," not understanding why it kept coming into my head. When I told Charlie, he spilled the beans.

Paul and I did have a few more good years together. We traveled with my family and played golf whenever he was able. The last time was a disaster, though, because he reprimanded me for not taking the game seriously.

On the seventeenth hole of Pomona Country Club, he shouted, "Damn you, Sis! You could be half decent at this if you would pay attention to what you're doing!"

I clowned even more as he did a slow boil.

Fast-forward ten years. My golf game improved and I earned a spot in the final rounds of the club championship. I played against my dreaded opponent many times in the league and she usually succeeded in intimidating me.

Life Takes Detours

Rifling through my closet to find a snazzy outfit, I heard Charlie's sarcastic mumble, "Wear strong perfume. She can smell *fear*."

At 7:30 AM, we were the first players on the course that day. I was wearing a brazen logo on my chest. The black T-shirt with large white letters announced, *"I didn't come here to lose!"*

The game was tied, until I won the sixteenth hole, which meant I had to hit first on the seventeenth. This was the same hole where Paul and I had our meltdown years before.

There, teed up, was a white ball sparkling in the morning sunlight. I reached down to pick it up, and it was the same brand Paul used every time he played—Wilson Square #1.

I was stunned. The tears came profusely. I couldn't hit the ball. I couldn't hit *any* ball. My opponent won that hole and went on to victory after the eighteenth. I walked straight into the clubhouse to show Charlie and our friend John.

Simultaneously, they shrieked, "That's Paul's ball!"

Julie McGlone

This warranted a trip to the cemetery. I hadn't been there since Paul was buried because I could not face his name in writing on the tombstone. But now I was *wild.*

"Damn you, Paul. You made me lose that tournament!" With golf ball in hand and shaking fist in the air, I must have been a strange sight for passersby. I didn't care. I had to clear the air. "Thanks for your good wishes, but you made me *LOSE!*"

Less than a month later, two of my other brothers died within days of each other. Then I realized Paul's message: nothing as trivial as a golf match. He was giving me a heads-up that he would be there to look after them. The comfort that gave me was priceless.

Tucked away deep in my mind, I have a picture of my mother and brothers reuniting. All of her chicks will soon be returning home.

In the House of My Parents

This has been the hardest chapter to write because the truth is not always funny. In many ways, this truth is not even pleasant. In my most sympathetic moments, I regret that I did not try to understand my father more when he was alive.

At the age of five, my father and his older sister Martha were separated from their parents and siblings as they arrived on a German ship into the United States. In the early 1900's, they grew up on the streets of Philadelphia with no positive role models. A few families would invite them in for Sunday dinner, though, and my father and aunt were grateful for the kindness of strangers.

In today's Internet society, someone could have found the lost family; but life was topsy-turvy for many orphans in that era. My father was a tortured soul.

He spent my childhood and most of his adulthood searching tombstones for evidence of his parents' demise.

7

Julie McGlone

On Saturday afternoons, we would drive
to the cemetery of the day. The searches were
always in vain.

Some poignant memories come to mind
when I speak about him. My siblings and I
looked forward to drives in the country, where
we enjoyed picnic lunches on the front porches
of strangers' homes. My mother would spread
out a clean tablecloth and pretend we were going
to buy the lovely houses with the "For
Sale" signs on the lawn.

One especially hot day, we packed our
bathing suits and drove to a lake. Admission
costs were higher than we could afford, but my
father brought part of his coin collection to add.
The gate attendant observed, "Sir, you must
want to take your family swimming awfully bad
to hand me those coins."

"Yes," my father replied sheepishly.
"Tell you what I'll do. I'll keep these
coins for two weeks and if you can come back to
get them, they're still yours."

We never swam at that lake again, but we did drive up to reclaim the coins, grateful for this empathetic employee. Our way of life was normal to us and we had nothing to compare it to. We never thought we were poor.

I remember walking to a health clinic whenever one of us was sick. The nurses would give my mother extra medicine, anticipating that the illness would prove to be contagious. And if the family doctor was summoned for a house call, my brothers and sisters and I would scatter to the farthest corners, never wanting to get the first needle. I can still hear my mother pleading, "Children, please come out. The doctor is a busy man!"

The only other time she would lose her patience was when we were roughhousing indoors. A football would be in midair or bodies would be rassling in a pile on the living room floor when we would hear her yell from the kitchen, "First one that gets hurt gets hit!"

First one that gets hurt gets hit! What kind of mothering was that? But it truly was effective crowd control.

9

I did not fear my brothers. I feared my mother's wrath when we had pushed her to the brink.

Christmas presented a challenge for my parents, as they tried to provide for nine offspring. At the stroke of midnight on Christmas Eve, we would survey the corner lot of discarded trees. All the customers and eager entrepreneurs had left the premises. We would strap the one we chose to the roof of the car and carry it into the house for adornment.

I remember our annual trip to a "children's home" where my father scurried out with packages, secretively placing them in the trunk. One open box revealed a doll's arm hanging limply over the rim. The doll was wearing a knitted blue dress and, when it appeared under our tree on Christmas morning, I knew to keep the secret and be thankful for what I got.

Aunt Martha's arrival often left us with conflicted gratitude. "Like those? A customer left them on my counter and I thought of you."

She was referring to the purple leather gloves I was unwrapping.

"Like that lamp? I found it in the neighbor's trash." This time she was addressing my mother, who couldn't find the words to thank her for the rusty metal lamp.

"You people are gonna miss me when I'm gone. If you're lucky, I'll remember you in my will."

This statement made the hairs on the back of my neck rise every time, and I purposely misbehaved so that I couldn't cash in on the contents of the will. But I was always glad to get the secondhand or thirdhand taffeta party dresses she harassed a friend for. They added a shimmer to an otherwise lackluster wardrobe.

During the student council food drive of my freshman year, I worked hard with my classmates to prepare baskets for the needy. We circulated flyers announcing we would be returning for canned good donations. We stacked, we sorted, and we drew cards wishing the recipients a happy holiday.

Julie McGlone

The cafeteria was filled with laundry baskets wrapped and ready to go, when the teacher in charge informed me I was not able to join the delivery team. How could this be? I worked just as hard as anybody else. I even took a box of rigatoni out of our kitchen cabinet so I could contribute. This was not fair. It was too late in the day to complain, but the next day I would voice my opinion.

So I walked home from school with my brother Paul, sulking and chewing his ear about how the teacher didn't like me. We were not in the door ten minutes when we heard a knock. There, on the lawn, stood upperclassmen who did not recognize us.

They held up a heavy basket filled with much better foods than rigatoni, as they sang, "We Wish You a Merry Christmas."

The teacher remained in the truck, but I would know that silhouette anywhere. I looked into his eyes during homeroom the following morning. We smiled and nodded. No other words were necessary.

We had another surprise one Easter, but this one wasn't as pleasant. My mother was in the hospital, and it was my responsibility to get the holiday outfits ironed and prepare the Sunday meal. Paul boiled the eggs and my younger brothers dyed them. It turned into a competition to outdo each other with messy tattoos and crayon markings.

Dad drove us to Mass and we paraded down the aisle. One by one, we took our seats. One by one, the eggs we had stuffed into our coats and pockets cracked with the impact of the oak pew. As the runny yolks dripped onto freshly ironed clothes, the colorful eggs stained our best secondhand attire.

It took every bit of determination we had to sit still through the service, and none of us was brave enough to walk up for Communion. We waited until everyone had left before slinking out to an impatient father.

What a treat it was to buy our school lunches one day a week—Hoagie Day. For thirty-five cents, we could smell like our classmates.

13

We chomped on PB&J the other four days; mine was usually tucked into a Wonder Bread wrapper.

My mother was a great cook. She could do more with a half pound of hamburger than anyone I know. I loved puttering in the kitchen with her, making cakes from scratch, using the mixer, or kneading the dough for homemade pizzas. We always spent the month of December baking cookies, but never seemed to have a plateful when the big day arrived.

As I talk about my mother, I realize that I am her. *I am my mother with opportunity.* She would have flourished in the richness of my life. She would have taken a chunk out of my gremlins' cheeks, kissing them with fervor. She would have a tear clinging to the corner of her eye, witnessing my grown daughters raising their families the way she wanted to raise me.

I remember her intelligence, her wit, and her eagle eye. She spent my childhood and adolescence warning me of unforeseen dangers.

At the age of twenty-eight, I became a motherless child; I was fully grown on the outside, vulnerable within.

After that, my father and Aunt Martha shared her house for almost twenty years. I continued to visit him, and on every visit, heard the same complaints from each of them.

"I can't stand that man another minute!"
"I can't stand that woman another minute!"

They died within twenty-four hours of each other. My father had such a peaceful look on his face. I wondered who was whispering in his ear as he left this world. Peace at last.

At that moment, I realized

the difference
between life and death
is
one
last
breath.

Julie McGlone

It was not until my father died at the age
of eighty-four that I was able to learn the fate of
his mother. She spent thirty-five years in a
mental institution, less than twenty miles from
where he grew up. There is no record of his
father's or siblings' deaths.

The Fledgling

When I retired, I left with a reputation of being a great teacher. Students, parents, and colleagues told me I had made a difference in their lives. My career began differently. In 1969, my salary was sixty-five hundred dollars and I was *not* worth every cent of it.

Wearing white gloves and black patent-leather shoes, I entered my second grade classroom—my Camelot for 180 days—with a feeling that this was my moment. I had *arrived*.

Within minutes, my crown was threatened. A note from one parent informed me that I was a heathen. Her daughter would be absent on Halloween and "any other time" we might be making preparations for a holiday.

"And don't force her to pledge allegiance," the mother warned. Forget the cocoon of a college classroom. *Welcome to the real world, Julie.*

As soon as the bell rang, one bright-eyed boy asked if he could speak to the class.

17

With a nod from me, he pulled a chair up to the board and drew all the planets with their identifying attributes. "I'm just going to leave you with one thought," he continued.

He drew the sign for infinity but never explained it to his second grade audience. I suspected that I was the only one who understood his message. On the way to his seat, he told me that his father would be in to see me at the end of the day.

Okay, so now I was batting 0 for 2.

I finished my first day in a conference with Boy Wonder's proud father. Gerald, I was informed, was unique; public education had not challenged his talents and curiosity. His dad doubted that I could live up to his expectations for his child. Moreover, he would let me know if I failed to treat his son with appropriate deference.

On day two I brought my little Emenee organ to accompany the class in my rendition of the national anthem. I thought my musical talents had gone over rather well, until later in the month, when one brave student raised her hand and pleaded, "Mrs. McGlone, do we *have to*?"

By the shocked look on my face, she knew she needed more ammunition. "The whole school laughs at us."

That did it. I walked out, Emenee in hand, vowing that these tone-deaf eight-year-olds would never bask in the glory of my musical prowess again. I asked the teacher next door to me to watch my class so I could take the organ to my car. He said, "That was *YOU*! I thought it was one of the kids."

Kick me when I'm down, why don't you?

Show and Tell—or as it was referred to in the faculty room, "Bring and Brag"—proved interesting as I sat in the back of the room watching the children show off their treasures. "This is my dad's favorite magazine. I found it in his desk" were the last words I heard before the child starting flipping through the magazine.

Julie McGlone

In those days, there was only one magazine that had a centerfold. I leapt over desks to grab it before the class could see Miss November in her full frontal nudity. This treasure surely could not go home in a backpack.

When I telephoned the father, he was just too busy to stop by that day. "Just send it home with Jimmy." The "Bring and Brag" stayed in my desk until I finally threw it out several weeks later.

Having no children of my own, I was a little harsh when it came to disciplining unruly students. On the first fire drill of the year, I would not let them go outside to the playground because of their noisy chatter.

Fortunately, the principal did not admonish me in front of the class. He just left a note in my mailbox.

"What were you going to do—let the Bluebirds burn?"

He was right. My reading group should have exited the building in case this was an actual fire. I never made *that* mistake again.

I also learned that some children needed more understanding than others. One boy would line up every day with the class to go to the lavatory. As soon as we returned to the room, he would ask to return to the lavatory.

I knew he wasn't bluffing, but just wanted to be sure. Again, I asked the teacher next to me to keep an eye on the class. I cracked open the boys' room door, eyes closed of course, and heard Billy's small voice singing "Little White Duck."

This incident has stayed with me because it reminds me that children are *children* first, not robots to be programmed and scheduled according to the mandates of the school.

Speaking of mandates, I dreaded the four observations every non-tenured teacher must endure. My classroom was running smoothly at this point, and the observation to me seemed like a dog and pony show.

Julie McGlone

When the principal walked through the door, clipboard in hand, pocket protector securely placed, my heart sank to the floor.

"Boys and girls, it's such a nice day. Why don't we go outside and enjoy the weather?" I chirped.

"But you told us we were bad and we would never see daylight!" they retorted.

Why couldn't these future delinquents just go along with it?

Smiling through gritted teeth, I claimed, "No, that was just to get you to try harder. Let's go!"

And out we strode, to the principal's chagrin. But he appeared on my doorstep the very next day, clipboard and pocket protector in full view.

"Boys and girls, let's line up for the lavatory." Clap! Clap! My hands assured them I meant business.

"But we just came back from the lavatory!" *These kids had no imagination.*

"I know, but we've been playing with art supplies and you know how important it is to have clean hands."

Off we marched, as the principal sat stymied.

By his third attempt, rain was pouring down outside, no art supplies were in sight, and I had run out of excuses. He sat in the back of the room and began recording every word I spoke. His face had such a confused look. When he noticed that all the children were wearing bedroom slippers, some knitted, others with animal heads as adornment, his expression was utter bewilderment. My own slippers were blue and fuzzy.

I did not get a chance to explain to him that the children could keep these slippers in their cubbies for rainy days. Since they walked to school, they would be extremely uncomfortable in soggy shoes. But I did not get a chance because—BAM! I fell right to the floor, overwhelmed by an anxiety attack.

To my recollection, he did an admirable job working with the class until I came to.

Now it was time to level with him. Now it was time to cut a deal. I would prove to him that I really could teach; I was just too nervous to have him nitpick my lesson.

The next day I brought in my Bell + Howell and set it on a table in the back of the room. At first the students were making faces and waving into the camera, until they heard the urgency in my voice. I proceeded through the lesson almost flawlessly. Then Billy Jean in the front row raised her hand.

"Yes, Billie Jean, do you have something to add?"
"Mrs. McGlone, I like the color of your slip."

Looking down, I saw the mint green slip hanging beneath my skirt. "Why thank you, Billie Jean. Any other comments?"

I looked around the room, holding my breath for other bombshells.

"That's it for today, boys and girls. Don't forget to do your reading assignment tonight."

When I finally viewed the movie production, I learned more in forty minutes than I had in four years of college. I saw myself turn my back to write on the blackboard too many times, I heard myself say "uh-huh" too many times, and the worst mistake of all was that I was always looking at the children who sat in the center row, straight ahead, instead of the ones on either side of the room. I missed a lot of eager hands by calling on the same students all the time.

One little devil actually took scissors out of his desk and cut the front of his hair while I was busy imparting my wisdom.

My principal went to his mailbox and found my tape with a note attached. "I learned that I have a lot to learn. The children may forget what I tried to teach them, but I hope they never forget the good things I try to do each day. Thank you for your patience."

25

From that day forward, he stopped by, walked around the room to see what the cherubs were engrossed in, and kept moving on.

By the end of the year, I suspect I was one of his favorite teachers—until I made the error of planning a class play. Costumes were handmade, parents were invited and actively involved throughout the process, and students could recite their lines in their sleep. The curtain went up and parents clapped at the sight of twenty-five children festooned and beaming.

Except for one little girl flushing her undershirt down the toilet during a costume change, the play went off without a hitch. We got a standing ovation for our elaborate production of *Winnie the Pooh Joins the Circus*. Cameras flashed, rave reviews appeared in the local paper, and I received a pile of thank-you notes from parents who appreciated that their children had been given such important roles.

I was Queen of the Faculty Room until the legal notice arrived. Some nitpicker in a Chicago clearinghouse was paid to catch honest citizens like me violating copyright laws.

Copyright laws? *Who knew*? Although the script was entirely original, I was not allowed to use the name "Winnie the Pooh" in the title or allow my students to portray any of the related characters. What Scrooges.

Before this latest offense, I had been offered a contract to return the following year. I could have tested the waters after the district settled the lawsuit out of court, but decided to leave of my own accord.

There was a rumbling in my tummy—my firstborn would be making her debut within the next nine months. From then on, she would become the star of my show.

Julie McGlone

Raising Daughters

I could separate them into two different chapters, but they'd do a word count to see who got more recognition. So let's start with my firstborn, Heather.

Nowadays we'd be more sensitive, but at the time it seemed like fun to have a pool on the exact date and time of the blessed event. Phone calls of cheers and jeers arrived at the beginning of the ninth month. Everyone wanted their share of the pot. When my body held out until long after anyone's expectations, I couldn't even answer the phone to hear the groaning on the other side.

Charlie and I were broke in those days. So broke that when our friends egged us on to have a New Year's party, I told him it had to be a "chip in"—every partygoer had to contribute.

At almost ten months pregnant, we invited thirty people over for the festivities. The food was prepared, the basement was decorated, but the host and hostess were not at home when the party started.

Dancing around the kitchen to the Twist and the Pony had propelled me into labor.

After several hours, the hospital staff told Charlie he might as well go home. These things take a while. Besides, I was in line to have the first baby of the New Year. *Big doings.* If the baby was the first one born in the state of New Jersey, a Cadillac was involved. If the baby was the first in the nation, the sky was the limit. In the maternity ward, I was the celeb of the moment.

Unfortunately, in the wee hours of the morning, someone somewhere beat me out of national acclaim. Then, another New Jersey mother claimed the first baby title for her little darling. Now I was small potatoes. Everyone on the staff treated me like a second-class citizen until my time came.

Then they passed my precious newborn into my loving arms.

"Oh, a boy!" I exclaimed.

"No, Mrs. McGlone. This is a girl. Sometimes newborns look like that, but she'll change."

With that, they bundled her in swaddling clothes and laid her in an incubator.

Charlie had been notified and he was on the way to the hospital with our friends. I remember seeing him galloping down the hall while my girlfriend was struggling with my heavy suitcase.

I was drowsy and battered from the maternal battle, and my first words to the new father were, "Did you get the money?"

"No, I forgot."
"Go back and get the money."

My knight in shining armor gave me a kiss on my sweaty forehead and walked down to the nursery to introduce himself to his bundle of joy.

Later that morning the nurse wheeled my daughter into my room. One look told me this was a mistake. I squealed. "This is not my baby! Where is my baby?"

I leaped from the bed and raced to the nursery, clutching the back of my hospital gown. There, waiting for me, in the incubator marked "Baby Girl Bennett" was my daughter.

Baby Girl Bennett? Was that the baby who took the New Jersey title? At the thought of losing my five-hour-old child, I picked Heather up and placed her in the incubator marked "Baby Girl McGlone," tears streaming down my hot cheeks. I had never felt so vulnerable in all of my life. *Welcome to motherhood.*

Heather and I had four years to get used to this motherhood thing before Lauren came along. Our daily routine included a walk into town, cooking something for Daddy, and reading or singing nursery rhymes. Housework was never an option.

Julie McGlone

Duchess, the family dog and Heather's loyal companion, insisted on accompanying her in the playpen or coach. Imagine the surprise and indignation of a woman who passed us on the street and asked to see the baby.

Heather and Duchess were tucked under the warm covers, braving the cold winter day. The onlooker pulled down the right half of the blanket, startling Duchess. The canine bodyguard sprang from the coach and chased the woman halfway down the block. I did not get a chance to explain that my little darling was resting comfortably under the left side. The woman never approached us on our walks again.

High on my newfound status of Earth Mother, I did not feel the need to justify my actions.

Duchess was the culprit in another drama. My mother-in-law had purchased a lovely smocked dress for Heather's first Easter. We were bustling out the door when Duchess refused to let Heather leave. Not meaning to hurt her loyal friend, Duchess grabbed the sleeve of the delicate dress and tugged.

32

The sleeve came off in her mouth, but it was too late to mend the dress.

Easter dinner was spent with Heather in her high chair wearing a spring coat. Every time the proud great-grandmother instructed me to take it off, I claimed it was too cold. I never got around to telling her the truth and managed to repair the silk sleeve before the next public appearance.

Life changed with Lauren's birth. Now I was outnumbered. That did not stop me from exposing my daughters to as many experiences as possible. It just made plans logistically more difficult.

The three of us enjoyed children's theater productions and often drove to the big city (not NYC, just Philadelphia) to attend them. Frazzled from the antics in the backseat, I often drove in circles trying to find a bridge—any bridge—to get home.

Julie McGlone

The newly constructed High Speed Line offered hope. I boasted to the giggling, excited girls that we would get to the city faster and I would lead the way.

One dollar and eighty cents bought us a round-trip ticket, but the railroad did not take paper money. I fed the grinding, noisy machine a dollar bill. Out came a coin that I thought was a quarter.

My intention was to show my offspring how to handle themselves in any circumstance. So I followed the directions that said, "In case of emergency, go to the window." The train was approaching and we were ticketless, so I hurried to the window.

"I put in a dollar and the machine gave me a quarter."

"You got a dollar," the matron said. Unfortunately the train station was so loud, I thought I heard, "You gotta holler."

"I got a quarter!" my voice projected.

"You got a dollar!"

"I got a quarter!" I shouted, still misunderstanding the attendant.

"You got a dollar!"

This clatter went on for several minutes with my daughters tugging at my skirt. "Ma, you got a dollar. See … this is a Susan B. Anthony dollar. That's what the machine takes."

Coins in the machine, we raced to the train. I pointed out several sites along the way, proving to them that they were in capable hands. The problem was I didn't know which stop to get off. Sitting nearby in his little conductor seat, the driver sensed this.

"You don't know where you're going, do you?"
"Yes, we do."
"Na-huh."
"Yes, we do. We're going to the Walnut Street Theater."
"Girls, do not get off this train until I tell you. And when I tell you, take your mother up the stairs to Ninth Street."

Ever the adult, I sulked until Ninth Street and then let my young daughters lead the way.

35

We did not have to travel far to find adventure, however. Adventure often came knocking. A trip to the grocery store, a challenge in itself, usually resulted in ultimatums. One time I bellowed, "If you two don't behave, we're going to leave this store!"

What was I thinking? That was the moment they had been waiting for. "Can we? Can we?" Rule #1 in *Being a Mother and Liking It*: Never make a threat you don't want to keep.

Arriving home from another grocery trek, the three of us spotted two wild dogs in our driveway. Although we lived near a forest, this was not an ordinary sight. *Think quickly. Think quickly.* What would their daddy do?

"Girls, this is the plan. It's getting cold and we can't stay in this car too long.

So, I am going to open the front door and come back for you." I said this with all the confidence I could muster.

"Mommy, those dogs! They look mean." I could hear the fear in Heather's voice.

"Everything will be all right. Trust me."

"M-o-m-m-y!" Lauren couldn't be convinced that I knew what I was doing. Neither could I.

Armed with a pack of fresh pork chops, I opened the door slightly and threw the feast to the dogs. Then I ran in the opposite direction to the door, unlocked it, and ran back to the car before the canines turned on me. *What could I throw? What could I throw?* Ah, the hamburger meat.

This time, I cracked the door open and gave my best outfield pitch. "Come on, Heather!" I gathered her and ran into the house. Furiously pointing to the front door, I demanded, "Do not open this door for any reason!"

Back in the car, the enemy was circling the Volkswagen. *What could I throw? What could I throw?* Ah, the steaks.

With Lauren in one arm and Charlie's dinner in the other, I cast the NY strips as far into the woods as I could. We made it to the door just in time.

"Girls, there's a lesson to be learned from this. Do you know what it is?"
"Call Daddy?"
"Call 911?"
"No, the lesson is that we are strong and we can solve any problem if we just think it through."

The remaining groceries stayed in the car until Charlie arrived. Meatless, we had a beautiful salad and Dinty Moore that night. Holding hands and saying grace, I thanked God for keeping my family safe and healthy.

Speaking of God, I should have listened to my daughters more. It would have saved embarrassment as I walked down to the altar for Communion. In my best holier-than-thou prance, I could hear one of my cherubs calling, "Ma."
I turned to give them both *THE LOOK*.
"Ma."
Again, *THE LOOK*.

"Ma, there's something coming out of your leg."

They were the last words I heard before looking down to see pantyhose peeking out of my pant leg and trailing behind me. The suck-your-tummy-in support hose had clung to my slacks during a washday frenzy. So much for a quick toss in the dryer. I leaned down in the most elegant posture I could muster and clutched the feet of the unmentionables in my hand. The priest never even blinked as he blessed me. He knew a lost soul when he saw one.

Times were tough when I was a stay-at-home mom, but they got even tougher when I took a teaching position in the school my daughters attended. As each of them entered seventh grade, I was the only social studies teacher in that grade. The only game in town. That meant Back to School Night and parent conferences with my husband. It also meant quiet nights at the dinner table when one of our daughters did not hand in *the homework*.

Seventh graders often act like they are at a masquerade party. They spend their thirteenth year trying on masks and personae, ever searching for the proper fit. My daughters were no exception.

The class was discussing war and peace one day when I leaned down and whispered to Heather, "Get in the girls' room and get that makeup off." I know she was trying to find herself, but she did not leave for school that day looking like Cher *in drag*.

One day a girl in my fifth-period class watched with great interest as I began my lesson. Her hand went up almost before I finished asking the first question.

"Yes, Kathy."
"Mrs. McGlone, you're wearing my sweater."

Now the whole class was watching with great interest. A minute ago they couldn't care less about world events; now I had their undivided attention.

40

"Kathy, I pulled this out of Heather's closet when I was getting ready for school this morning."

"Yes, and she pulled it out of my closet when we agreed to switch clothes for a week."

Flabbergasted, I knew the only way to diffuse a situation with teenagers was with humor. "Well, next time could you loan her something pink? I look better in that."

During election years, the social studies class prepared debates, posters, and campaign materials for our mock election. The camera was rolling when I recited the rules for the debate and instructed each team to take its side. Heather stayed in her seat as the class moved into position.

"What are you doing?"

"I want to be Lyndon LaRouche."

"Yesterday you wanted to be a Democrat. What happened?"

"I just changed my mind."

And so the debate began. Democrats versus Republicans versus Lyndon LaRouche. Heather dazzled them with the facts. Her air of confidence and ample materials won the votes of most of the class. Only a few complained, "That's no fair. She knows what she's doing!" I did not agree with her political choice, but applauded her right to make it.

When both girls had graduated from elementary school, I thought my troubles were over. Ignorance is bliss, isn't it? I had no idea what was in store for me.

One day, a student stopped me in the middle of a lesson and said, "Mrs. McGlone, Lauren was driving the school bus yesterday."

"Now, Phil, you know that isn't true, so please don't start rumors."
"She really did," several others chimed in. So much for class participation.
"She drove my brother and our neighbors," the saga unfolded.

I don't remember how I kept myself calm to finish the lesson, but as soon as I could get out of the building, I headed over to the high school.

From the look on my face, the secretary knew to put me through immediately. The principal was browsing through *Field and Stream* and did not lift his eyes when I entered the room. Then he muttered a casual, "Hi, howya doin'?"

"Not good. My daughter drove the bus yesterday."
"Now, let's not exaggerate."
"My students told me about it. She escorted their family and friends home."
"Sit down and let's talk."

A few days later I asked Lauren if anything was happening on the bus.

"The old man isn't there anymore. They have a new driver."
"Rumor has it that you drove the bus one day."
"Yeah, but he let the fat girl drive more."

Of course a lecture on unlicensed bus driving ensued, but I never did confess to having the driver fired. Some things do not need explanation.

Raising children is like being pecked to death by a duck. You just bandage the wounds and limp forward.

Dirt versus Memories

Charlie prided himself on taking his family and our friend John to wonderful vacation spots each year. He started planning the itinerary during the winter months, with the AAA guidebooks and maps taking up most of the dining room table.

I was always grateful for his enthusiasm, but usually complained that we needed landscaping, a deck, carpets, or general house repairs. Money was tight. I am glad now that he ignored my years of whining.

When he announced we would be flying to Las Vegas and driving to the Grand Canyon, I made a mental note to look up all the hazards that might befall us on the road trip. Snakes were a biggie. I read about how to identify snakes and how to release the venom should one of them bite me or my cherubs. I was prepared.

We stopped at several photo ops, posing at the edge of steep inclines, asking passersby to click on our cardboard camera for posterity.

Julie McGlone

Charlie and John returned to the front seat of the rented station wagon; Heather and Lauren hopped in the back.

Off we went to the next itinerary highlight. This routine was interrupted when one of the girls inquired, "Where's Mom?"

The car squealed to an abrupt stop, and the astonished passengers looked out the back door to see one of my legs in the door, with the rest of my startled body outside. I probably was dragged only ten feet, but my skin was bruised for the remainder of the vacation. And you know that I insisted on being the photographer because black and blue just aren't my colors.

Before my daughters left the nest, we had driven and flown to at least forty states and several countries. It gives me great pleasure to see them now raising their families with the same zest for travel.

It gives me greater pleasure when I see museums on their itineraries, even though there was a time when my teenagers complained, "This trip was supposed to be fun. Dad's trying to educate us."

Dad did educate all of us in the value of bonding through unique experiences. I have all the photos in boxes, not scrapbooks. I just have to inspect the scenery or daughters' hairstyles to be swept back to the adventure.

Julie McGlone

Hearts Across the Water

In the fall of 1991, Russia was a country in limbo. The Communist government had to make way for a new democracy, but the people were hesitant to learn new ways. What if this was only temporary?

Twenty-four American teachers were invited to work with Russian counterparts in an effort to usher in the new era.

To get to Nizhni Tagil, a city in the Ural Mountains, we took a ten-hour one-stop flight to Moscow, a two-hour domestic Aeroflot plane to Sverdlovsk (now called Yekaterinburg), and about a three-hour bus ride to meet our host families.

The only information I had received about Lena was an unsmiling photograph and reassurance from the organizers of the teacher exchange that the two of us would be a "good match."

Life Takes Detours

There was very little small talk on the walk to my temporary home. What had I gotten myself into *this* time? Lena, her husband Andrew, Babushka (Andrew's mother), and their two daughters, Anya and Natasha, lived in Babushka's one bedroom flat. A six-foot mastiff, a cat, a white mouse, and a bird also shared the living quarters.

Andrew carried my bags up five flights into the bedroom. I was to sleep alone in the double bed, while the rest of the family sprawled out elsewhere. I hardly slept at all, though, realizing that I had disrupted this family's routine.

By the second day, Lena confided in me that the government insisted she fix up her flat with new wallpaper, bed and table linens, and a toilet. She was to be reimbursed for the project, but so far the check was not in the mail.

She also asked several poignant questions about life in America. The first one startled me, but sensing her sincerity, I knew better than to joke.

49

"Julie, is it true that Americans take smiling lessons?"

"No, Lena."

"Our government told us that if we ever saw a picture of Americans smiling, they were practicing their smiling lessons that they had learned in school."

How do you begin to tell a person her government lied? You just keep a poker face and let her do the talking—at least until you get to know her better. It was at that moment I realized why I had never seen her smile. Her mouth was full of gold teeth, not the white billboard smile of an American.

"Andrew and Babushka are angry that I would invite someone to see how we live. And my colleagues are afraid you will go back to America and laugh with your friends about our schools."

"Lena, you are a very brave woman to sign up for this exchange. I think this is the beginning of a very dear friendship."

It did not take long for us to become confidantes after she told me what was at stake for her marriage and her reputation. We enjoyed long, gossipy girlfriend talks about husbands, daughters, and mutual careers. Lena especially enjoyed the fact that no one in her house understood English, so she could speak her mind while nodding to the family.

On my third day in Tagil, it was time to start my teaching duties. A car had been parked outside the apartment house since my arrival, and now the driver was ready to take me wherever I needed to go. When I asked Lena why he just sat there for the first two days, she was puzzled.

"Why not? He gets paid whether he drives or not. It is the Communist way."

We had gone several blocks when I noticed that we were circling the same building over and over again. A nod from Lena told him to continue around the block. Finally, I just had to ask.

"Is there a problem, Lena?"
"Yes, the principal is not finished painting the school and we cannot embarrass her."

There, on the front steps of the school, was a woman in a black dress, high heels, and pearls, with a large paintbrush in her hands. She was putting the finishing touches on the white columns. I promised Lena that I would not touch the wet paint or make eye contact with the principal until the paintbrush was tucked away.

As I was escorted into her office, I realized this very distinguished-looking woman spoke no English. I smiled my best I'm-in-your-country-with-good intentions smile and gratefully ate the cheese and sausage offered.

Two students entered with a large bouquet of brilliantly colored flowers and a loaf of fresh bread and salt. I was prompted to dip a piece of bread into the salt as the others followed the ritual.

Lena and I walked through the halls with all eyes on the foreigner. I commented to her that the lace curtains on the windows and hanging plants on the walls made the building look very inviting. She replied that students were required to bring in a plant on the first day of school, choose where they would hang it, and take care of it for the remainder of the year. Students were neatly dressed, boys with dark blue jackets and girls in uniforms with large white bows in their hair.

All the students were wearing their Lenin scarves. These red neck scarves with a picture of Lenin printed on them were required under the Communist government. No one had given the students the nod that it was safe to come to school without the scarves.

Eager students spoke beautiful textbook English in the classes I attended. My voice surprised them, however. "Julie, your intonations! They have never heard someone speak with such excitement."

Throughout the days, I witnessed lessons on Shakespeare and other English authors. Students played the piano in classrooms as others read aloud. Chemistry and geometry lessons in the seventh form were much more advanced than my American students had been challenged to learn.

Without the benefit of modern technology I had come to depend on, it seemed that teachers in Lena's school had been doing just fine. The only difficulties I noticed were in social studies classes as the teachers tried to explain why the government had changed and why former heroes had lost their status.

At the end of each lesson, a student was designated to sweep the classroom. The students cleaned the cafeteria tables and floor at the end of each lunch period, also.

When I told my American students about this practice, they said, "No wonder the school was so nice! They knew they had to take care of their own messes!" *Enough said.*

One morning in the principal's office, I decided to tease Lena.

"Lena says that you are a very strict boss. She thinks you should let her work less and go home to her family earlier."
"Julie, she does not understand you."

"Precisely, Lena. I can tell her anything I want to and so can you."

Picking up the cue, my new friend berated her superior in English for past grievances, smiling at her the entire time. Lena and I had just discovered a new game we could play.

Becoming comfortable in our relationship, we could also joke about the two worlds we came from. As we arrived home each day, boxes of food would be on the doorstep or already stacked in the kitchen by Babushka.

"Julie, what kind of food is this? I have never seen it before. My government wants you to believe that we eat like this all the time."

I made the mistake of throwing out Natasha's chewing gum while cleaning the dinner plates one night. She wailed relentlessly as Lena explained that children are given one piece of gum and it must last the whole week. I reached into my pocketbook to get her a new one, while promising not to spoil her. I wanted my American students and even my American family to appreciate what they have, and at that

precise moment I realized how obscenely I lived
in my life of disposable goods.

The government supplied Lena's family
with a toilet, also. Before my visit, they just had
a hole in the floorboards, which led to a pipe
five floors down. I asked Lena why there were
so many locks on her door.

"Do you have a problem with burglaries?"
"We are afraid someone will steal the
toilet."
"Has that ever happened in Tagil?"
"Yes. The thief dragged the toilet down
several flights of stairs and was stopped by a
policeman on the street. He was sentenced to
thirty years in prison."

Evidently the judge felt the punishment fit
the crime.

A press conference was scheduled for the
second week in my trip. At least five hundred
Russians were crammed into an auditorium to
ask me questions with Lena as the interpreter.
She reminded me that the KGB would be present
and not to speak ill of her country.

I answered as honestly as possible, looking out at the sea of faces. The buzzing audience grew quiet and I could see that many people had wet faces.

"Lena, what is the problem?" I whispered out of the side of my mouth.

"The problem, my dear, is that they expected to hate you. You are the face of the enemy they never saw."

With that, I laid down the microphone and walked down into the audience. I reached my hand out to the people and they reciprocated. We smiled and cried together. The government of these fellow humans had caused me to hide under my desk during air raids at school. Neighbors built bomb shelters in fear of their arrival. And now we were hugging.

A wedding reception in Tagil was like none I had ever attended. Fish head soup was the first course and guests had to "rent" the spoons to help the bride and groom pay for the festivities. When everyone insisted that the American should get the fish eyes, I explained that in my country the bride and groom were more important and deferred the honor to them.

A live chicken flew overhead and the guests bid on it to add more to the newlyweds' finances. Then it was time for the bride to prove how hard she would work for her husband. Everyone dumped the cloth bags of papers and trash they had brought for the bride to sweep. The groom had to climb on the shoulders of two other men to reach the paper money, which had been tacked to the ceiling. What an industrious couple!

Andrew was such a conscientious host. When a man approached our table, asking me to dance, Andrew would stand, shake the stranger's hand and speak to him. After several dances, I commented to Lena that the Russians were such gentlemen.

Lena laughed and confided, "That is because they have been told if they try to touch you, Andrew will hurt them."

I felt safe everywhere we walked in Tagil.

One day I noticed that a policeman and guard dog had been walking twenty meters behind. When I wanted to thank the man, Lena warned that he was doing his job. I should not recognize his efforts.

Closing ceremonies for the teacher exchange brought mixed emotions. Most Americans were glad to be returning to the comforts of home. But I'll never forget the comments of one man, "When I get home I will have to be the person everyone expects me to be. The American personae. Here I could let down my hair and enjoy whatever happened."

We boarded the bus the next day, while clouds burst into a loud downpour.

"You brought women's summer!" the Russians called out. "Now we are back to our dreary ways."

As Christmas approached, I warned my family not to buy anything for me. My house was already full of too many material goods. I told my friends about the unique experiences I had, knowing full well that they thought I was exaggerating. Lena would be arriving in the

59

spring and they would meet this very brave woman and love her as much as I did.

In April 1992, friends, family members, and colleagues at my school prepared for the exciting event. Students made a large sign for the front of the school: "Strasvitzia, Lena!"

Luncheons and dinners were planned so that everyone would get a chance to speak with her personally. This was her fifteen minutes of fame. Boy, did I miscalculate.

The train trip and flight were so strenuous that Lena arrived with an ear infection, chest congestion, and a severe case of anxiety. She spent the first two days in bed, with my husband and daughters checking on her and bringing soup or tea. The mention of a doctor brought on a stubbornness I had not seen in Tagil.

"He will put me in the hospital! I will be there for a month! I cannot go!"

Now we understood her perspective. I called the family doctor and explained that she needed to make a house call in the guise of a friend. "Jo Ann" arrived without the black bag and white coat.

She empathized with Lena and suggested that Lena take a medicine that had worked well for her. This was a big white lie, but it got my Russian friend on her feet and socializing—until we got to school.

The sight of the beautiful building, along with a sea of smiling faces sent her reeling into the nurse's office to sleep on the cot for the first day. I could not rush this process just because I had been foolish enough to think we were going to have a smooth visit.

It was time to meet our friends the following week. Restaurants caused even more trauma, though. The menu was foreign to her— not the language, but too many choices of foods she had never known. When I would ask, "What would you like?" the reply was always "Whatever you're having, Julie."

When Lena saw the food that was served and the food that was cleared from the tables she would cry out, "This is food my family will never see! Julie, please can we go home?"

The social schedule was adjusted once again so that we could eat at our house or the homes of family or friends. But the temperature was always too cold for her.

In Tagil, the furnace blasted day and night at eighty-five degrees. In America, we kept our heat and air conditioning at a much lower temperature. Lena would shiver until the hosts obliged.

Then came the gifts. When someone presented her with a beautifully wrapped package, she would acknowledge it with a thank-you and put it under her coat. At home she admitted that she could not open anything in public because she did not know how to unwrap it and she would appear foolish if she did not know what it was.

This did happen when our friend gave Lena two beautifully embellished Christmas stockings for her daughters. While I was out of the room, Lena took off her boots and tried to squeeze into them. They were halfway up her calves when I suggested that we take them home to examine them further.

As the weeks went on, students and teachers at my school enjoyed long conversations with the reluctant celebrity. In an eighth grade assembly one afternoon, she was fielding questions and surprised all of us with frank responses.

Someone asked, "How do you like life in America?" And everyone, including me, expected her to regale on its beauty.

"Julie, can I tell the truth?" she asked out of the side of her mouth.
"Tell it like it is, kiddo."
"You live in Paradise." At this the audience smiled knowingly. "But you don't appreciate it. You wear gold jewelry and expensive sneakers, yet you always ask for more."

In her best teacher voice she has startled the students and staff who anticipated other answers.

63

Lena returned to her country with three thousand dollars appliquéd into her blouse. Everyone who met her loved her. Friends and family members slipped the money to me so that she would not be humiliated.

At the appropriate time I presented her with the garment and warned her not to mention it to anyone on the trip home. She knew exactly what to do with the windfall.

On the three-day trip to America, Russians practiced their English and had nightmares that no one would understand them. On the trip *back* to Tagil, the Russians practiced their Russian, fearing that they had forgotten it in their new environment. What would their colleagues and families say?

Seven days later I called Lena. "What did Andrew say about the money?"
"I haven't told him about it yet."
I guess I taught Lena more than I had planned to.

Three weeks later, she called to say, "Julie, I took the shirt to the bank. I cut it open and deposited the money so I could buy a farm."

She always wanted a summerhouse so that she could grow vegetables for her family. The farm was in her name, the only time in her life when she possessed something of her own.

Charlie and I returned to Tagil that summer and the trip turned out to be everything I promised. He had the best and worst time of his life. Lying in bed the first night we arrived, he asked, "*What were you thinking?* We almost got killed getting here and everyone's sleeping all over the living room because of us."

"I forgot how difficult it was. But I did know how important it was to Lena to show her friends that we would come back again."

Babushka was the bouncer who would decide who could cross the threshold to meet the Americans. Sometimes intruders were met with a ferocious "Nyet!"

Other times they joined us for the evening, feasting on a variety of cocktails.

Charlie is such a finicky eater—no fish eyes for him—that I packed cans of tuna and a jar of peanut butter. But when I saw how thin the mastiff and the cat had become, I treated the animals to a bountiful feast. That meant a hungry husband for twenty days.

When Lena's friends asked what he would eat, Charlie thought of the easiest thing to make - pizza. With some dough, cheese, and crushed tomatoes, the Russian men and their new friend Charlie started a makeshift pizzeria. That satisfied his taste buds.

Just as we had made plans for Lena's visit, so she had made great efforts for our trip. We went on a rowboat ride across a large lake to picnic on the other side. Everyone had to leave their passports at the rental office. This was customary for the Russians, but Charlie and I were a little nervous about never seeing our tickets out the door again.

Laughter, songs, and delightful chatter rang across the lake as we made our way to the other shore. Our rowboat was not navigated by the strongest man, so everyone pointed and laughed, howling, "Zigzag! Zigzag!"

Badminton and swimming were the main entertainment, but when Charlie brought out jars of bubbles for the children, the adults went wild. They blew bubbles and danced like two-year-olds. And this is what I remember most about our trip—childlike laughter at life's simple pleasures. I wished that Americans could put down their video games and just breathe in the moment.

Lena and her friends also took us on a three-hour train ride through Asia to a summer rest house. We played cards and formed a conga line on the train, dancing from car to car. We hopped down from the train and carried our bags down the path. We were greeted by several goats to which Lena exclaimed, "The barbecue has come!" Dinner that night consisted of freshly made salads and various goat parts.

Charlie had become one of the guys at this point. The men knew he was a good sport and capitalized on this. They carried him from the dinner table, stripped off his outer clothes, and tossed him into a slimy indoor pool. Then they placed his shivering body next to the fireplace and beat him with birch branches. Grown men squealing "Banya! Banya! Banya!" is another sound I will never forget. I was glad the women understood that I was not such a sport.

The final step in the banya ceremony is a trip to the icy river. The men carried Charlie's wriggling body and tossed him in like Raggedy Andy. But to everyone's amazement, he was so energized that he ran back to the house to repeat the process.

What a showman. My hero. It made their trip worthwhile.

On our last night in Tagil, all the men stood on the balcony of Babushka's flat and sang "We Shall Overcome" in their native languages.

They emerged in the living room with tears in their eyes. We danced and sang until our car arrived late in the night to take us to the domestic airport in Yekaterinburg.

Six-foot-six Andrew sat in the front seat of the compact car with the driver, while Lena, Charlie, and I sat in the back holding suitcases and gas cans we would need for the trip. After two hours of fast driving, the driver yelled what must have been profanity.

"What's the matter, Lena?"
"We have a flat tire. It is just a small matter." So the driver yanked tools from the trunk and repaired the tire with a wing and a prayer.

One hour later, we heard another profanity.
"What's the matter, Lena?"
"We are going the wrong way."

At that point Charlie and I knew our fates were in the hands of this stranger and there was nothing we could do about it.

We both slept from exhaustion and, thankfully, woke up at the airport the next morning.

Lena and Andrew accompanied us on the Aeroflot flight, and Charlie and I had made a pact not to show surprise over anything the Russians did. But when we went through baggage claim in Moscow, we were met by two thugs who wanted to shake us down. "You pay or you stay."

Charlie was reaching for his wallet as I was sticking out my chin and my worst attitude to inform the men they were crooks. As if they didn't know.

"You pay or you stay," they repeated.
"No! Who do you think you are? You can't get away with this!"
"Julie, this is no time to pick a fight!" Charlie yelled.

With that, he threw them three twenty-dollar bills and the four of us ran outside while the Russian guards just watched casually, awaiting their cut.

We had booked two rooms at a beautiful hotel, knowing that Andrew and Lena had never stayed overnight in Moscow before. The rooms were reserved in our name and when the hotel staff saw two Russians walk through the door, they said Andrew and Lena could not stay. Charlie and I were appalled.

"If they can't stay, we won't. And we have spent a great deal of money for this hotel."
The reluctant clerk disappeared and conferred with the management. He returned to say that the hotel would make an exception this time.

On the way to the fourth-floor rooms, Lena spotted a camera in the elevator. She began making faces into it. I'm afraid my new BFF was mimicking some of my disrespect for authority.

At dinner that night, Andrew realized that he had forgotten his room key. This could have been solved at the front desk, but he didn't mention it.

71

As Charlie and I walked up to the buffet, we saw a man climbing up the interior balcony walls.

"Lena, what's Andrew doing?"
"He forgot the room key. He will be okay."
Patrons and the McGlones gasped at each grip on the balcony railings until Andrew reached the correct room. Lena was cool as a cucumber. This was not the first time her knight had singlehandedly solved a dilemma.

Lena and her family visited the United States several times. Our friends became her friends. My family embraced her family. On the last trip she brought eight Russian students who lived with eight of my students. By all accounts, this was a huge success.

My son-in-law bought her a large backpack to carry her gifts from the Tagil train to her home. He strapped it to her back as she began her astronaut imitation, "That's one small step for man, one giant leap for Lena." She galloped about weightlessly.

Yes, my dear, the whole experience has been one giant step for my brave friend Lena.

On the last day, all the families met at my house to drop off the students and share a final meal together. We stood outside my house and sang "We Shall Overcome." Most of the Americans had tissues in their hands.

When I was accompanying Lena and the students back to JFK Airport, the mood in the van changed from somber to lighthearted. The students began speaking in English and changed to Russian. They loved their new friends but looked forward to returning to the homeland they understood.

When someone joked, "Americans don't use their ovens," I laughed heartily to let them know that it was okay to poke fun at my culture.

In hindsight, I suspect we learned more from the Russians than they could learn from us. But I must admit that neither Charlie nor I can get through "America the Beautiful" without feeling a tightness in our throats.

Julie McGlone

And the title of the exchange program "Hands Across the Water" could easily be substituted with "Hearts Across the Water."

Nuggle Me, Jammy

"What greater thing is there for human souls than to feel that they are joined for life to be with each other in silent unspeakable moments?"   George Eliot

Lauren's son Tim and I have bonded since the first time I held him. Most evenings ended with one request, "Nuggle me, Jammy."

Tim called me Jammy for at least five years until he became a worldly, sophisticated kindergartener.

One time he asked, "Did you hold me a lot when I was little?"
"Absolutely."
"I thought so, because I can still remember the sound of your heart beating."

I hope that sound is embedded in his memory when I am no longer around to hold him close. It is the sound of two souls connecting.

During an emergency room visit when he was two, the attending physician inquired, "Did he have a bowel movement today?"

"Yes. It was perfect."
Dr. Youngstud rolled his eyes and replied, "Spoken like a true grandmother."

As the firstborn grandchild, he was the beneficiary of my latest, greatest tunes and antics.
You've got two eyes ...
Two legs!
You've got two ears ...
Two legs!
You've got one nose ...
Two legs!
Yes, that's right, Tim. You've got two legs
...
You've got one chin, but what a chin does nobody ever knows ...
Two legs!

Having finished dressing my one-and-a-half-year-old sidekick to the tune of a *Sesame Street* song, I stood him up, and he fell flat on his face.

76

I had pushed two legs through one pant leg, missing all his cues. I was too busy congratulating my future Broadway star for helping me with the song.

Then, of course, there was the obligatory crawl through a McDonald's playground tube when he was three. Most of the tube was plastic. When I saw other children enjoying themselves through the maze, I did not want him to miss the experience.

Off he raced, looking backward to make sure Jammy, his comfort zone, was following. Halfway through the journey, he noticed that I was stuck in the tube and could not proceed forward or retreat backward.

Quiet tears, then outright wailing signaled our distress to restaurant onlookers. I will be forever grateful to the quick-thinking mother who sent her daughter into the tube through the exit. The smiling four year old was able to convince Tim to follow her out to safety. As for me, I did not have a charming escort. The manager helped dislodge me. Oh well, we made it.

Heather's son Patrick arrived on the scene when Tim was six years old. I felt that I had to make a point of telling Tim he was still number one.

But one day, when I whispered, "You're my favorite person in the whole world," he countered with, "That's not fair to Patrick. You have to love him, too, Grammy."

And when I whispered, "You are my best boy," to Patrick, he whispered back, "Grammy, that's not fair to Tim. He is your best boy, too."

That epiphany made me realize I was outnumbered by my loving gremlins.

Of course there are many occasions when that old demon jealousy rears its ugly head. It did with my daughters. It will with their sons.

"See that? I made it for Grammy," Patrick boasted.
"See *THAT*? I made it for Grammy," countered Tim.
"See that ..."
"See that ..."

The rivalry of two grandsons perched at my kitchen table, snacking on our freshly baked treats, continued. Out of artifacts to brag about, Patrick defiantly continued. "Poppy is taking me to the pumpkin patch."

Not to be outdone in this battle of one-upmanship, Tim coolly responded, "Poppy doesn't like pumpkins."

Tears, squealing, and hurt feelings of the younger cousin ensued until the referee stopped the match.

"Gentlemen, Poppy and I love both of you. Tim, you are my favorite person in the whole world. Patrick, you are my best boy in the Milky Way Galaxy."

I turned toward the sink and heard Patrick having the last word, "To infinity and beyond."

Hands held around the Thanksgiving table, Tim was instructed to say the grace.

"Dear God," he began.

"God! Where's God?" Patrick questioned. He jumped under the table in search of God. "God, are you under there?"

Tim joined him eagerly. The tablecloth was moving and the glasses were shaking when I yelled, "Everyone come out from under the table and eat your food, dammit!"

"Potty talk! Potty talk! Grammy's talking potty talk."

Yes, I was. Desperate times call for desperate measures. But I have not used potty talk since then.

When Patrick was celebrating his birthday at a local nature center, the conversation went something like this:

"Come see the snake!" Patrick invited.
"No, I can't see the snake," I replied squeamishly.
"Come see the turtle!" he negotiated.
"What a great turtle," I applauded.

Thirty minutes later, Miss Cathy, the party coordinator, arrived and announced that she would bring any snake out of its cage for Patrick's guests to touch.

"No, please bring out a turtle," Patrick whispered.

THAT boy is in the will.

I've tried hard to be a good mother, but grandmothering just came naturally. Patrick, Tim, Katie and I often operate in an imaginary world without the boundaries of logic. I lovingly refer to them as my gremlins.

There are props to play with, art supplies to splash in, and musical instruments to summon for our entertainment of the moment. We danced and marched publicly and privately to recorded songs or our own originals.

One of my favorites was "Mr. Golden Sun, Please Shine Down on Me," which had to be performed on my front porch in our best Al Jolson voices and choreography. We could have been booked as Grammy and the Gremlins, and now Katie has joined the folly.

Tim, at ten, was reluctant to join in. "Grammy, I'm older now."

He may outgrow the fun, but *I know I won't.*

The gremlins have been my kitchen helpers since the day they could walk. They would push a chair up to the counter, climb onto it, and observe whatever recipe I was making. It just took a signal from me for them to know which measuring cups, spoons, or ingredients they would be in charge of.

Holidays and family dinners became a chance for each of them to show off their culinary skills, complete with aprons and chef hats. Of course, I help them choose their offerings carefully so that each one will get an equal number of "oohs" and "aahs."

Patrick has a sense of social consciousness far beyond his years. One night we had gone through the usual bath/book/bed routine and I was zipping through the prayers, desperately wanting to rest my own tired bones.

"Dear God, please keep our family safe and healthy," I began.

"G-r-a-m-m-y," he stretched out the name to emphasize his opinion.

"Grammy, there are other people who need God's help, not just our family."

"You are so right, Patrick. Dear God, please bless all the people in the world."

"G-r-a-m-m-y, there are people who have too much water. I saw it on TV. God needs to help them."

My budding social worker/missionary/TV commentator finally closed his eyes and snuggled with me when I got the message right. "Dear God, please help the victims of Katrina and please keep their families, friends, and everyone else in the world safe and healthy."

"Thank you, Grammy."

Katie was born in 2008. I have loved her since she was thumbnail size in my daughter's womb.

Overwhelmed with wishes for her bright future, I pray she will be healthy and safe. Her big brother Patrick made her a beautiful pink Build-A-Bear with a snuggly pajama outfit. Given the opportunity to choose an additional outfit, he examined every item for just the right one—a T-shirt with a picture of the planets on it.

"I want to show Katie what planet God sent her to," he explained.

Katie doesn't need my good wishes. She has a remarkably kind and sensitive big brother to be her tour guide through life. God bless them both.

As a grandmother, I try to foresee future dangers; I feel that I absolutely must point out any hidden traps so my heirs apparent can avoid them.

"Button up, you'll catch a cold."
"Don't jump off those high monkey bars. You'll get hurt."
"Never talk to a stranger, especially if he or she stops a car to ask if you've seen a dog."

I always end with, "You're too important to me."

Patrick doesn't skip a beat. "You're too important to me, too, Grammy." And this declaration lets me know that we have a deep connection to carry us through into a future we cannot see.

Julie McGlone

Passion

Marriage is a dance. And most women of my generation have spent their marriages dancing backward. Then one day the high heel breaks and that Peter Finch phrase, "I'm mad as hell, and I'm not going to take it anymore!" gets personal. We'll mow down anyone or anything that gets in the way of our plans.

Who is this man and why is he calling me "Wife"? Charlie, my husband of so many years, steps out of the shower, body red-hot from the steam and clumps of gray hair sticking out from his chest and scalp.

Somehow I focus and can still see that eager young man who courted me. He has given over forty years of his life to his family, generously and lovingly.

But I know the secret to keeping him happy. When the rest of the world goes away for the night, I acknowledge his presence. I understand that deep down inside he just wants to be appreciated; that little boy inside every man still needs approval for a job well done.

Besides, I gave him the skinniest years of my life. Where can I go from here?

That's why I was so outraged when he was having a seizure at our favorite family restaurant, Buca di Beppo. (The gremlins love it there because they can draw pictures on placemats for the waiters to hang in the kitchen.)

Charlie had been quiet through most of the meal; his silence went unnoticed in the chatter. I thought he had stepped outside for fresh air, until the receptionist shrieked in a loud voice, "Some old man is on the sidewalk!"

"That's my old man!" I announced. "Call 911!"

Heather and Lauren raced outside and pulled him up to a bench. They were holding him and pleading, "Wake up, Dad. Come on, Dad." They rocked him gently, hoping for a response.

I arrived onto the scene, pushed them aside, and started shaking Charlie mercilessly.

"Don't you *do* this to me!"

After a few minutes, he started coming around.

"Mom, don't ever become an EMT," my son-in-law suggested.

Rick had left Tim and Patrick with the waitress at the table, where they were revising their drawings of hot spaghetti. Instead of "Buca, we love you," the captions read, "Get well, Poppy!"

The rescue squad arrived as I was fishing the credit card from Charlie's wallet.

"Mom, get in the ambulance," Heather directed me.
"No, you go. I'll follow behind in the car."

As the driver was pulling away, I changed my mind. I yanked open the passenger door and told Heather to get out. At this point, the dispatcher came across in a crackly voice, "What seems to be the problem? Why haven't you left yet?"

"They keep getting in and out of the ambulance," the driver reported.

"Tell them to get their act together and get the patient to the hospital!"

With this, I knew to sit up straight and behave. The situation was out of my hands.

When we arrived at the emergency room, the triage nurse asked what medications Charlie was on. I was so proud that I remembered he kept the list in his wallet. I handed it to her and returned to his bedside.

"When did he start taking Aricept?" the nurse came in to ask.

"He doesn't," I corrected her. (I've heard horror stories about hospitals and this was shaping up to be one.)

"That's what it says on the card you gave me."

"Oh, that's his mother's medicines. Let me find *his* list."

At this point I lost all credibility with the people who were most crucial to his recovery.

Shortly after that, a doctor overheard me whispering to Charlie, "You are the most important person in my life. You are my warrior."

The young intern called me outside the cubicle to warn, "You are putting too much pressure on him with a statement like that. Just let him rest."

I agreed to let him rest, but it was important to let my husband, lover, friend, and warrior know just how much he meant to me at that moment in time. And I hope the doctor finds this kind of passion in his life.

Charlie was my caretaker, nurse, and housekeeper when I was recuperating from major surgery several years ago. He organized the kitchen, kept the cereal in alphabetical order, vacuumed, and folded the wash late at night. I was completely relaxed and satisfied to hand over these responsibilities. Our daughters were very young at the time, so the burden fell on him to cook the family meals.

One of them came into the bedroom and whispered to me, "The house isn't burning, Mommy. It's just Daddy's cooking."

He drove me to my five-week checkup and waited in the parking lot. Forty-five minutes later I returned to the car, closed the door, and quietly mumbled, "The doctor said one more week, Chall."

Back to bed and fluffy pillows. Back to no housework or wash.

Several years later I fessed up. The doctor actually said, "You're as healthy as a horse. You can go back to your usual routine."

Yes, Charlie accompanies me into appointments now.

To keep spontaneity in the relationship, I often plan surprises for Charlie. One of the infamous ones was an impromptu trip to Myrtle Beach. His secretary was my accomplice. She knew I would arrive early on a Friday afternoon, bags in the trunk, and whisk him to the airport.

No appointments were scheduled and his car would remain in the parking lot for four days. With a kiss on the forehead and a motion to get into the car, he was wary of leaving the reins in my hands.

"Where are we going?"
"Just a little trip to break up your winter."

He still had a startled look on his face when we walked through checkout at the airport. Midflight, he really started to beg for information.

"Where are we going? Just tell me that."
"Hilton Head."
Now the other passengers began whispering among themselves, "Hilton Head? Are we going to Hilton Head?"

I did not want to say Myrtle Beach because our friends were there at the time and this would ruin the second half of the surprise.

As we left baggage claim, we could see four smiling faces awaiting us. The two men had crutches and fake casts on their arms and the two women held up banners cajoling Charlie into giving their husbands more strokes on the golf course.

The surprise was a success. We had a ball. There was only one tiny error on my part—I forgot to pack his shaver, contact lenses, and pants. In my haste I had packed four days' worth of Lauren's slacks, which meant they both had wardrobe malfunctions.

Another secret to my happy marriage is time away from each other once in a while. Yes, absence does make the heart grow fonder. When Charlie took his employers to conventions, I was a free woman.

On his first night away, I was always glad to lie comatose on the sofa with sour cream and onion potato chip crumbs falling from the corners of my mouth. By the second day, I could feel a little twinge, a bit like heartburn, but I still enjoyed being the queen in my castle.

On the third day, loneliness would kick in. I decided he should know this.

As I was getting dressed for work at 7:00 AM, I called the hotel to tell my warrior how much I missed him. Groggy but pleasant, he listened as I rambled. I proceeded to tell him my plans for our rendezvous when I got to the hotel that night. *Explicit* plans.

"This is a helluva wake-up call, lady."
"You're not Charlie McGlone!"
"I never said I was."
"Then why didn't you stop me?"
"I wanted to hear what you were going to say next."

I slammed the phone down and redialed the front desk. Finally connected to the room where Charlie was staying, not just a room he had booked for his employers, I told him how angry I was at the anonymous man.

"You didn't tell him my name, did you?"
"Of course I did."
"You should have just hung up without saying who you were."

Click was the next sound Charlie heard. That night I drove to the hotel and endured an embarrassing dinner, with the anonymous man seated across from me. There were ten of us at the table, but he and I could not make eye contact all night.

Since then, I have demanded secret codes and inside information before any phone conversation. In my most paranoid moments, I will not even take the dead bolt off the front door until I hear a social security number or the name of his first pet.

Charlie asked me to drive home one night after an evening on the town, and I ran over the concrete parking divider, thinking it was a speed bump. I did see the policeman who was supposed to be discreetly watching patrons after they left the establishment, however. He pulled out after me and followed three cars behind, as if I wouldn't notice. This made me so nervous that I bobbed and weaved, trying to keep his whereabouts in my rearview mirror.

After several blocks, he decided to declare himself with a flashing red light.

"License and registration, please."

"Officer, I know what you're thinking, but I was not the one doing the drinking."

"Ma'am, just give me your license and registration, please."

"Look at him; he's in no condition to drive. So I was going to get us home safely."

"Ma'am, step out of the car, please."

"No, I won't step out of the car! I've heard about fake police who make women do that."

Fumbling for my license, I ripped the plastic off my wallet.

"Now, look what you made me do. You made me nervous and I ripped my new wallet! You should be following drug dealers, not citizens like me."

Rooting through the glove compartment for the registration, I pushed all the contents onto the floor. "Look at this! My registration is in this pile somewhere, but I can't see it in the dark. You know I have one! Are you a former student of mine? Do I look familiar to you? You know I would not break the law and you are making me nervous!"

"Ma'am, I can see that your eyes are clear, so I can assume you have not been drinking, even though your behavior is erratic. I'm going to let you go with a warning this time."

"Thank you, Officer. How old are you? I have a daughter you might want to meet."

"Thank you, Ma'am, but I'm already spoken for. Drive safely now."

I started the car and crept down the highway. Charlie mumbled, "Menopause must be wonderful."

Before I get to the serious stuff, here's a little humor for my married friends:

A woman, standing nude, looked in the bedroom mirror and said to her husband, "I feel horrible. I look fat and ugly. Pay me a compliment."

The husband replied, "Your eyesight's damn near perfect." He never heard the shot .

And now for young wives, old wives, and any women who just want to hear what this hausfrau has to say—this is what I have learned:

Julie McGlone

I am glad God didn't give me everything I asked for. My cup is already overflowing.

Love may be blind, but lingerie is still a staple in a happy household.

Love is *friendship on fire*. Don't settle until you feel the *heat*.

Finally, to quote my husband and best friend, "We began together and we'll end together. Everything else is just a speed bump in between."

He just *had* to mention speed bumps.

On the Road Again

Our family is grown now, but my daughters still worry when we are traveling. They keep in touch via e-mails and the cell phones they bought us. These e-mails recount a few of our adventures …

Hawaii   February 2006

Only glitch on the flight was me falling asleep and waking up screaming. It startled the passengers and stewardess, but Dad just pretended he didn't know where it came from.

Driver met us in LA and we watched the baggage carousel go around at least twenty times before realizing the airline had lost our luggage on a nonstop flight. That's tricky.

Your father patiently walked to the lost baggage office and methodically gave the contact info if it ever showed up. I, on the other hand, was a wild woman. When the lady said, "Name one article in the suitcase for identification purposes," I bellowed in my best hyena-on-crack voice, "IMODIUM!"

Julie McGlone

Then we got to the hotel and I tried to check us in while Dad and the driver were smoking their asses off. The puny little clerk behind the desk said, "Oh, I have bad news. We are overbooked. We will send you to another hotel and give you complimentary dinner and drinks."

Blood pressure medicine has long worn off, so I leaned over farther and growled, "Make them alcoholic!"

After two straight vodkas—the waiter sensed my state of mind.

At the hotel, I rolled on top of the covers with my clothes on. When Dad started to pace about the situation, I mumbled "Thatshhs okay," and fell into a coma.

Shaky start to a dream vacation. But all has turned out well. Luggage arrived early AM to the wrong hotel and they kept it for us. Love to all of you.

Later in the trip, I tried to reassure our daughters that their father and I were responsible adults:

Your father is trying to kill me. Yesterday, ten of us rented a 4WD van to go two miles down into the valley on a one-lane dirt path.

When we got to the starting point, the straggly, foreign looking driver was under the van fixing it. Then he walked around it shaking his head and finally jumped the batteries. Conversation inside went like this:
"I think he's drunk."
"I think he's stoned."
"I think he's a hippie."
"I think he's Cajun."
"Where did the blood on the windshield come from?"

And the lady with all the jewelry from New York kept whining, "Is he going to feed us lunch? I thought they said we would get lunch." (Take my word, she didn't need it.)

Then he got into the van, started it, and said, "Hi, folks. How is everybody?"

Julie McGlone

How embarrassing. He could understand every word we said.

His three dogs ran in front of us, alongside, and behind all the way down and back up. Happy dogs.

Today, we took ATVs on a twelve-mile- six up and six down- winding path through cow pastures and up into the mountains. The owners of the 2007 Kawasakis and I came to a mutual agreement that I should not be driving my own, so I rode with the guide.

In case Dad does manage to bump me off, I hide all my money in the ..."

Yes, I left the whereabouts of the family fortune out deliberately.

Mom's Travel Blog
October 2007—Driving to Florida

Friday- *I was dozing on I-95 when I noticed your father was having one of those seizures. I was mentally planning how to take the wheel, when he mumbled, "Need salt or sugar."*

Both of us hugging the wheel, we barreled toward the nearest exit. We went into a store and bought peanuts and candy bars and stuffed them into his mouth. Five minutes later we were good to go.

I drove to dinner that night. Three screams (your father's) and three blocks of terror later I raced into the parking lot of a private trucking company. The guard was not amused.

Saturday- *After we made reservations for the evening, it took us three phone calls to get more directions because we were lost. I was in full throttle when I told Dad to pull over because the cell phone faded.*

We got out of the car to get better reception, while a fire engine was honking

*behind us. We did not notice the smoking
building in front of us.*

*We found our way to the hotel and I
checked us in while Dad stood outside. As I
stood at the front desk, I noticed a curly phone
cord stretched to the max and I heard a
whispering voice say, "We have a situation.
Come NOW!"*

*The sweet young thing behind the counter
was watching my eyes get bigger as I listened to
the mystery voice. She said, "Don't be alarmed.
This happens all the time."*

*I went outside and said to Dad out of the
side of my mouth, "Get in the car."*
"What?"
"Get in the car."
"What?"
"Why?"
"THE COPS ARE COMING!"

*The delinquents in the parking lot ran like
roaches when the light comes on.*

After dinner I came back to write this on the lobby computer, but things got too exciting. Still frisking people for guns, underage drinking, and illegal drugs.

Sunday- *We are back in golf cart captivity. Love to all of you.*

P.S. Don't look under the guest room bed. I will get that stuff in November.
P.P.S. Don't look in the den closet. I will get that in December."

Charlie and I were getting back into the retirement groove when we enjoyed a meal at a local restaurant one evening. I was carrying a beautiful alligator handbag my friend Donna had given me.

It drew compliments wherever I went, but almost got ruined on this fateful night. I raced into a restaurant bathroom and waited patiently in a line of women.

When it was my turn, I found that the only stall unoccupied was the handicapped one. So I placed my designer purse in the sink and

105

perched on the throne five feet away.

As I assumed "the stance," my eyes were drawn to the sink. I witnessed in horror as the automatic faucet released a quart of water into my handbag. As soon as I was able, I reached my hand into the sink to rescue the waterlogged purse. Too late. The water started rushing again, sensing the motion of my hand.

I placed the pile of squishy leather on the floor and washed my hands. But by this time, the automatic sensor on the toilet didn't know whether to flush or not. Technology is wonderful when you can keep your mind on it.

Exiting the stall with the small dignity I could muster, I heard one do-gooder in line accuse me, "You're not handicapped."

"No, but I was in a hurry."
"It's against the law to use the handicapped stall if you're not."
"What are you, the bathroom police?"
Nice intelligent comeback. Just keep walking, Julie.

So I flung open the door and swaggered to my table splashing patrons to and fro. They were casualties in the bathroom wars.

Charlie, ever the romantic, questioned with wide eyes, "What did you do now?"

I just gave him *THE LOOK*.

Julie McGlone

Blue

Cancer took the lives of my mother and four siblings. I used to have a dream that I would be walking home from school with a figure of death closely behind. I'd walk faster and finally reach the porch of my parents' house. *Safe.*

But a few minutes afterward, I'd get sidetracked. When there was a knock on the door, I'd open it. Death would stand there waiting.

Blue is the color of a sentinel node biopsy. And when you hear the diagnosis, the noises in the room around you become muted, inaudible. You can only hear the one word you dreaded. *Cancer.* You stare at the doctor, pretending to comprehend his instructions. Unless he can get inside your mind, he does not know that your world just turned upside down. From that moment on, you realize just how fragile life really is.

Is this my final detour? Time will tell.

Life Takes Detours

I chose this memoir to give my final instructions, just in case.

Never write an ordinary obituary for me. My life has been anything but. With family and friends and a life of purpose, I was a millionaire.

The day before yesterday, my twin brother Paul and I enjoyed funny, sunny days at my uncle's farm. We romped and rode on tractors, standing on tippy toes to reach the most luscious peaches at the top of the trees.

Along came my knight. He held my hand at Dingle Bay, Lake Como, the Blue Lagoon in Iceland, the birch forests of Siberia, and several other spots on the globe.

Charlie is my lover and protector of forty-some years, with whom I share dreams and count blessings in late-night talks.

Two daughters who probably arm wrestled each other to get this diary first are everything I prayed for. Some days I had to pray extra hard. Both smart and beautiful and loving.

Julie McGlone

Two grandsons and a granddaughter—the precious stones in my crown, the reason I need no other jewelry to adorn me—are usually attached to my hip. I look into their bright eyes and see possibilities.

They complete my circle of life.

Today my mother will hug me and whisper, "Good job."

I hope Paul made it to heaven. I can't wait to see the look on his face when he laughs, "You again!"

Never cry over a life well spent. God took special care of me.

Love you, love you.

Sis/Julie/Mom/Grammy

Made in the USA
Charleston, SC
19 September 2014